Johannine Writings

I, II, III John

K.W. Bow

Copyright 2016 by Kenneth W. Bow.
The book authors retains sole copyright to his contributions to this book.
Published 2016.
Printed in the United States of America.

All rights reserved.

No portion of this book may be reproduced, stored in a retrieval system, or transmitted in any form or by any means – electronic, mechanical, photocopy, recording, scanning, or other – except for brief quotations in critical reviews or articles, without the prior written permission of the author.

ISBN 978-1-9860028-9-2

Front cover design by Mark Gauthier.

This book was published by BookCrafters,
Parker, Colorado.
bookcrafterscolorado@gmail.com

This book may be ordered from
www.bookcrafters.net and other online bookstores.

Foreword

Thank you reader, for selecting my book. There are many choices of books and we all have a limited window of time to read. I appreciate you purchasing my product. It is a humbling thing to know someone would choose to purchase, and then read your work. I do not take it as a small matter. By purchasing and reading a book, the reader and the author form a certain bond as they travel a road together for a short time. It is especially rewarding when the two agree on the content. It is my hope you can find inspiration and life challenges in the pages of this small booklet.

From the days of my high school years I have found the Bible fascinating. I have travelled to Israel on two occasions to learn more about the land and culture of the Bible. I worked on an archaeological dig and lived on a Kibbutz to better inform myself of how to understand this book from God. I have read it from cover to cover over twenty times, and it is still as exciting to me as it ever was.

The Bible is a magnificent journey and experience. It is ever a delight. In it you will travel to distant lands and meet some of the most incredible people of history.

It will introduce you to kings and peasants. You will walk the palace halls of castles and the open fields of the countryside. You will meet the famous and be introduced to people whose name we will never know. You will read some of the greatest love stories ever told and you will see the dark side of man as the evil manifests itself in heinous ways. Every emotion of man is highlighted at some time. You will see greed and avarice and murderous covetousness. You will also see the greatest examples of love and sacrifice that mankind has ever contributed. For indeed the Bible is the story of man. It is the whole story, and nothing is left out or omitted. It is the ultimate mirror of life.

When we invest time in the Bible we indulge a bit of the eternal. The Bible will never pass away, even in the eons of the future. If you have read it sincerely then my hope is this small work will intensify your understanding and enjoyment a little more. It is the grandest journey we can make while in this life. Thank you for sharing a portion of your life journey with me.

Kenneth Bow

Table of Contents

1 John..1
   Chapter 1..5
   Chapter 2..11
   Chapter 3..20
   Chapter 4..25
   Chapter 5..30
2 John..35
   Chapter 1..37
3 John..43

1 John

Introduction. He lived in Ephesus. He was now an old man in his late eighties or early nineties. He was the last of the surviving apostles that Jesus had hand picked. He was also Jesus' cousin. Over sixty years before he and his brother James had been standing by the fishing boat their father owned. Jesus had walked by and said come follow me and I will make you fishers of men. John left the boat and began a journey that was now over sixty years later.

The years had been incredible. For three years he had followed Jesus while the messiah taught and ministered to thousands. John had been selected by Jesus to hold a special place along with his brother James and Simon Peter. These three men were the inner circle to the ministry of Jesus of Nazareth. On several occasions Jesus had taken these three men into confidential moments the other disciples did not share.

John had been there for the entire journey of Jesus earthly ministry. He was at the foot of the cross when Jesus died. John had been there through all the years of the New Testament church. John was right there on the first day of the church in Acts two. He was there when the lame man was healed. John was with Peter when they were cast into prison. He had been there when his brother was martyred by Pilate. John accompanied Peter to the house of Cornelius in Acts chapter ten. John had lived through the destruction of Jerusalem in 70 AD. John had been at the Jerusalem council when the decision was made for the Gentiles entrance into the church. The years were filled with memories of triumphs and tragedies.

Now he was the last original surviving apostle. He was feeble and aged. Troubling news was being brought to him about false teachers who were teaching false doctrine. This was a growing epidemic in the church. Gnosticism had gained a foothold, and taught that Jesus never really had a human body. This false doctrine said the flesh was intrinsically evil, therefore Jesus would never have inhabited such a sinful abode.

No one on earth was better qualified to rise up and refute this false doctrine that threatened his beloved church. The old apostle picked up his quill and with shaking hand began, "That which was from the beginning, which we have heard, which we have seen with our eyes, which we have looked upon, and our hands have handled." John was refuting Gnosticism directly. He was letting the churches of Asia and Europe know, I was there. I saw him. I touched him. I was his companion for three and a half years. John was proclaiming I saw it, and I bear witness, and show you eternal life.

Jesus was manifested to mankind. John was declaring that all men can have fellowship with Jesus Christ.

Thus begins the first general epistle of John the beloved.

Date: 90 ad

Author: John

Place: Ephesus

Chapter 1

1.1 That which was from the beginning, which we have heard, which we have seen with our eyes, which we have looked upon, and our hands have handled, of the Word of life;

1.1 Eyewitness. John begins by assuring the churches of Asia and Europe he was an eyewitness of the ministry of Jesus Christ. John was offering his personal witness of the word of life, which is the proclamation of Jesus Christ, in whom is life. This parallels his statements in chapter 1 of his gospel, and gives weight to his authenticity. John is the most qualified witness on earth as he is the last remaining original apostle. All other original apostles are deceased, thus unable to raise their apostolic voice in dissension to false doctrines circulating in the church.

1.2 (For the life was manifested, and we have seen it, and bear witness, and shew unto you that eternal life, which was with the Father, and was manifested unto us;)

1.2 Manifested. Manifested here means to render apparent, declare. The life of God was rendered apparent in the life of Jesus Christ. Jn 1.1 mirrors this, in the beginning was the word (logos), and the logos was with God and the logos was God. Jesus is the manifestation of God to mankind. 1 Tim 3.16 without controversy (by the consent of all), great is the mystery of godliness (gospel scheme). God (theos, the supreme deity, spoken of the only and true God), was rendered apparent. God lived in the human body of Jesus Christ and made Himself apparent to mankind.

1.3 That which we have seen and heard declare we unto you, that ye also may have fellowship with us: and truly our fellowship is with the Father, and with his Son Jesus Christ.

1.3 Fellowship. One important purpose of John's personal witness is to provide fellowship for true believers. The most insidious way false doctrine invades the church is through men posing as sheep but are actually ravening wolves, Mt 7.15. Fellowship here means partnership, social intercourse, and communication. This is the root of what John is defending. Men posing as true believers were interacting with the church and bringing damnable doctrines with them. John is rooting out fellowshipping these false believers. John is firm: you are not to have close association or relationship with people who do not believe Jesus was God manifested in the flesh. The Apostle Paul also declared this in his writings. One important platform of fellowship is mutual acceptance, and submission, to the truths of the Christian Faith.

1.4 And these things write we unto you, that your joy may be full.

1.4 Joy. The major purpose of this epistle is to defend the church against the false doctrines trying to invade the fellowship of believers. There is a secondary benefit in the joy (cheerfulness, calm delight), that comes with close fellowship with Christ and other believers. There is a deep satisfaction in knowing Christ and walking with him.

1.5 This then is the message which we have heard of him, and declare unto you, that God is light, and in him is no darkness at all.

1.5 Light and darkness. John relays the message he heard from Jesus personally as an eyewitness. This message he passes on to the fellowship of believers. John introduces the first of his comparative opposites, light verses darkness. This is a writing style of John. He uses simple words that have great meaning. John's vocabulary is the vocabulary of a seven year old child. He uses roughly 600 words. A child learns 100 words a year on the average. The words John uses are few in number but pregnant with great meaning and impact. The clarity of his style is effective. For instance, where there is light there can be no darkness. This simple style is his signature trademark in the Holy Scriptures. God is light. There are only two things in the scriptures that say what God is. God is light and God is love. All other statements are about God's attributes. In the beginning God said let there be light. God introduced himself into the darkness and creation began. It is the same pattern in a life. When God is introduced through the baptism of the Holy Ghost, light and illumination begins. The Holy Ghost will teach things, illuminate things, and bring things to a person's remembrance. God is light and light illuminates and drives darkness away by its very presence and existence.

1.6 If we say that we have fellowship with him, and walk in darkness, we lie, and do not the truth:

1.6 Fellowship. Walking in darkness means walking in sin. People who claim to be a part of the fellowship of light but continue to walk in darkness (shadiness or obscurity), utter an untruth (lie). This type of lifestyle is simply impossible, for light will drive out darkness.

1.7 But if we walk in the light, as he is in the light, we have fellowship one with another, and the blood of Jesus Christ his Son cleanseth us from all sin.

1.7 Blood. John introduces another of his simple yet profound words, blood. If we walk in the light we have fellowship with one another, but more importantly we have the continual flow of the cleansing blood of Christ. The blood of our body flows without stop or rest. Our blood is the blueprint for the redeeming, cleansing blood of Christ. His blood flows continuously in our lives to keep us free from sin and death. To truly understand this revelation is to live above guilt and condemnation. While we live daily lives, Jesus blood continually flows in our life to keep us spiritually healthy. John now introduces the reason why this is important.

1.8 If we say that we have no sin, we deceive ourselves, and the truth is not in us.

1.8 Sin. We must acknowledge sin in our lives. If we

deny we have sin, we live in deception, and truth is not in us. There were possibly some who were claiming to have no sin because of the life of Jesus now inside them by the Holy Ghost. John clearly instructs, all people sin. Jesus taught if you acknowledge your sin you can find forgiveness. He further instructed if you are blind to your sin you will remain there (Jn 9.41).

1.9 If we confess our sins, he is faithful and just to forgive us our sins, and to cleanse us from all unrighteousness.

1.9 Confess. To confess (assent, acknowledge) our sins, is to seek help from God to remove this death virus from our spiritual man. In God's providence, when we acknowledge our sin, his continuously flowing blood removes our sins. He is faithful (trustworthy). As our blood continually removes metabolic waste and impurities from our body, so His blood does for the body of Christ. His blood goes even further by cleansing all unrighteousness (injustice, wrongfulness of character or life) of the body of Christ. This is one of the reasons the Apostle Paul stressed the importance of the church to not forsake the assembling together (Heb 10.25). There is cleansing for the spiritual body both individually and collectively when the church gathers together.

1.10 If we say that we have not sinned, we make him a liar, and his word is not in us.

1.10 God. To deny one's sinfulness or sins does not just deceive oneself, it makes God a liar by denying God's word. Sin is universal. It was brought into the world by Adam and Eve in the garden of Eden. It was finally conquered at Calvary by Jesus Christ. To be sin free is impossible. The answer is for the blood of Jesus Christ to continually flow in our lives daily, much as our natural blood does, to remove sin when it occurs. John will now introduce the amazing concepts of advocacy and propitiation.

Chapter 2

2.1 My little children, these things write I unto you, that ye sin not. And if any man sin, we have an advocate with the Father, Jesus Christ the righteous:

2.1 Advocate. An advocate is an attorney who represents a client in a court of law. This is the ministry of Christ today. He speaks in behalf of his children when they sin. It is natural for a parent to defend their children. Here Christ uses His blood and righteousness to defend the believer's failures and sins. The goal of a believer should be to overcome, not simply confess. We are admonished to sin not. The Greek word for advocate has a twofold meaning. It means intercession and consoles. While Christ intercedes to the Father, He simultaneously consoles the child of God. This word also holds a connotation of comforter. Christ comforts a believer who has failed. His advocacy is directed to the Father and also to the believer.

2.2 And he is the propitiation for our sins: and not for ours only, but also for the sins of the whole world.

2.2 Propitiation. This means to expiate or atone. Expiate is to extinguish the guilt incurred by the sin. It also means to put an end to. This ministry of Christ is exemplary in that He removes all guilt to sins we commit and then puts an end to it. Christ is the advocate and the propitiation for our sins.

2.3 And hereby we do know that we know him, if we keep his commandments.

2.3 Obedience. John says we can and should "know"Christ. This Greek word ginosko, is a prolonged form of a verb and is used in a variety of applications. If a believer truly knows Christ, the believer will be obedient. This is the signature mark of truly knowing Christ.

2.4 He that saith, I know him, and keepeth not his commandments, is a liar, and the truth is not in him.

2.4 Liar. John boldly declares anyone who claims to know Christ and is disobedient is living a falsehood. Light and darkness cannot coexist, neither can truth and error. One of these will ultimately drive out the other.

2.5 But whoso keepeth his word, in him verily is the love of God perfected: hereby know we that we are in him.

2.5 Perfection. One of the major teachings of Jesus was obedience. The end of obedience is perfection. The believer cannot reach perfection on their own, but the act of simple obedience brings perfection. Perfection in this context means accomplish or consummate or finish.

2.6 He that saith he abideth in him ought himself also so to walk, even as he walked.

2.6 Walk. To abide or stay in Christ requires that the believer walks as Christ walked. The basic call of Christianity was simply to take up the cross and follow me. To follow Christ and walk and abide in Him requires to walk as he walked. This does not bring perfection, it is the result of obedience.

2.7-11 Brethren, I write no new commandment unto you, but an old commandment which ye had from the beginning. The old commandment is the word which ye have heard from the beginning. 8 Again, a new commandment I write unto you, which thing is true in him and in you: because the darkness is past, and the true light now shineth. 9 He that saith he is in the light, and hateth his brother, is in darkness even until now. 10 He that loveth his brother abideth in the light, and there is none occasion of stumbling in him. 11 But he that hateth his brother is in darkness, and walketh in darkness, and knoweth not whither he goeth, because that darkness hath blinded his eyes.

2.7-11 Love and hate. John illuminates the issue of love verses hate. He does so by using the powerful image of light and darkness. This is not a new commandment. This was introduced as a new commandment by Jesus in the upper room on the night of the last supper, Jn 13.34. John returns to this commandment now. John calls this an old commandment. One definition of old here is worn out. No doubt over the last sixty years since Jesus introduced it, this commandment had been worn out in keeping peace in the body of Christ. Love and light are interlinked. Hate and darkness are bound together. To hate is to be in darkness, and walk in darkness. Hate (miseo), is to detest or to love less. The warning here is that when in this state of darkness, a believer cannot see where he is walking. Hate blinds a believer to walk in the light. The effort to walk and follow Christ becomes obscure.

2.12-14 I write unto you, little children, because your sins are forgiven you for his name's sake. 13 I write unto you, fathers, because ye have known him that is from the beginning. I write unto you, young men, because ye have overcome the wicked one. I write unto you, little children, because ye have known the Father. 14 I have written unto you, fathers, because ye have known him that is from the beginning. I have written unto you, young men, because ye are strong, and the word of God abideth in you, and ye have overcome the wicked one.

2.12-14 Age groups. John addresses different age groups to reassure them of their security in the faith. This distinction of various age groups may be literal age or it may refer to levels of spiritual maturity. New Christians may be referred to as children.

2.15-17 Love not the world, neither the things that are in the world. If any man love the world, the love of the Father is not in him. 16 For all that is in the world, the lust of the flesh, and the lust of the eyes, and the pride of life, is not of the Father, but is of the world. 17 And the world passeth away, and the lust

thereof: but he that doeth the will of God abideth for ever.

2.15-17 Love not the world. Light and darkness cannot coexist, love and hate are opposites. A believer cannot love God and love the world at the same time. World here does not denote last humanity, for we should love sinners and unsaved people. The connotation here is to not love the world system that will pass away. The lust of the eye, the pride of life, and especially the lust of the flesh will all pass away. These are the gateways into our spiritual man and can eventually cause us to be lost if we do not hate them. Idolatry can take many forms in different ages and societies. This overarching principal is universal and must be applied to each locality and worldly temptations. Each person is tempted in different ways according to their individual weaknesses. Temptations do follow a general pattern for all believers. The temptation will use one of these three gateways to tempt believers to sin. Our key weapon against these temptations is the word of God. This is the weapon Jesus used in His hour of supreme temptation. Modern day temptations of Hollywood movies (lust of the eye), professional sports venues (lust of the flesh), and fellowship with unbelievers (pride of life), are examples of temptations from this world that must be hated and not loved. Early Christians did not attend the Roman games and gladiator contests. The early church was aware they were citizens of another country, and they were just passing through this world on their destination of a heavenly city. This mind set must be formed in a child of God to insure the believer does not love the world, neither the things that are in the world. To love the world is to have the love of the father absent in our spiritual temples. The lusts and temptations of this world are passing away, and this leads to the conclusion that it is the last time and antichrist is appearing soon.

2.18 Little children, it is the last time: and as ye have heard that antichrist shall come, even now are there many antichrists; whereby we know that it is the last time.

2.18 Antichrist. Antichrist appears only here and in verse 22, 4.3, and 2 Jn 7. Antichrist is the ultimate opponent of God, God's plans and God's people. The prevalence and abundance of false teaching causes John to remind believers they are in the last days and the spirit of antichrist is among the true believers. These are former believers who were once part of the assembly. Their leaving and refuting their faith proves they were never truly part of the true church. Their fruits prove what tree they are of.

2.19 They went out from us, but they were not of us; for if they had been of us, they would no doubt have continued with us: but they went out, that they might be made manifest that they were not all of us.

2.19 True believers. Some had gone out of the assembly of true believers and departed. This holds true today in Christianity. Many appear to be religious, but are not true believers. Jesus proclaimed in Matt 7.15-21 that there would be people who claimed to be His followers and would claim to have done many mighty works in His name. Jesus proclaims He never knew these that claimed to be His followers. Outwardly they appeared to be Christ's, but they were imposters. Christ sends them away. John is here reminding the true church there will always be the spirit of antichrist in the world.

2.20 But ye have an unction from the Holy One, and ye know all things.

2.20 Unction. Unction means anointing or unguent, or smearing. A true believer has this unction. They are covered or smeared with the Holy Ghost, and this comforter, the Holy Ghost teaches a believer all things, Jn 14.26.

2.21-22 I have not written unto you because ye know not the truth, but because ye know it, and that no lie is of the truth. 22 Who is a liar but he that denieth that Jesus is the Christ? He is antichrist, that denieth the Father and the Son.

2.21-22 Liar. The liar here is the deceiver who claims to represent Christianity, but actually opposes it by their false doctrine. This is probably directed at the Gnostics of John's day. These teachers denied Jesus His full deity and thus took away His full due as savior and as God manifest in a human body. This eternal truth and warning is relevant today. Anyone who denies Christ is less than divine and not God manifest in the flesh is a liar. This is the key identifying trait of antichrist, the opponent of the messiah. This title antichrist is only used by John. Some apply this term to the man of sin mentioned in Paul's writing and the evil leader who arises in the last days described in the book of revelation.

2.23 Whosoever denieth the Son, the same hath

not the Father: he that acknowledgeth the Son hath the Father also.

2.23 Son. God has chosen to reveal Himself through Christ. It is impossible to know God without acknowledging Jesus Christ in the fullness of His power and purpose. To deny the son, is to deny the father.

2.24-25 Let that therefore abide in you, which ye have heard from the beginning. If that which ye have heard from the beginning shall remain in you, ye also shall continue in the Son, and in the Father. 25 And this is the promise that he hath promised us, even eternal life.

2.24-25 Abide. This powerful word speaks of a continuing life in Christianity. Believers are exhorted to stay, to continue, to endure, and to remain. The charge is to persevere in the face of false teaching. This is in contrast to those who had departed and fallen from grace. The reward for all who abide is eternal life.

2.26 These things have I written unto you concerning them that seduce you.

2.26 Seduce. John boldly proclaims he writes because of error and false teachers invading the church.

2.27-29 But the anointing which ye have received of him abideth in you, and ye need not that any man teach you: but as the same anointing teacheth you of all things, and is truth, and is no lie, and even as it hath taught you, ye shall abide in him. 28 And

now, little children, abide in him; that, when he shall appear, we may have confidence, and not be ashamed before him at his coming. 29 If ye know that he is righteous, ye know that every one that doeth righteousness is born of him.

2.27-29 Anointing, abide. John provides the method for believers to abide. It is the anointing that provides the ability to discern false teaching. This anointing reveals false teaching. John is not saying a believer never needs teaching. John is affirming the anointing, which is the Spirit of God, will teach you all things about, and when, deception rises and tries to invade the church. False teaching does not agree with the true spirit of God the believer has abiding in their heart. The anointing will teach you when false teaching tries to gain a foothold in the assembly. This anointing will in turn cause the believer to abide until the coming of Jesus Christ. A true believer will meet Jesus Christ at Christ's return with confidence and joy.

Chapter 3

3.1-2 Behold, what manner of love the Father hath bestowed upon us, that we should be called the sons of God: therefore the world knoweth us not, because it knew him not. 2 Beloved, now are we the sons of God, and it doth not yet appear what we shall be: but we know that, when he shall appear, we shall be like him; for we shall see him as he is.

3.1-2 Bestowed. When a person is born again that process of sonship continues. This is a prolonged form of the verb here meaning bestowed. Believers are the sons of God and continue to be without interruption. John reaffirms believers are now the sons of God and we will follow Christ's pattern when Christ returns. Believers will become what Christ is. All true believers are in the process of becoming like Christ. This comes from abiding in Christ as John referred to in the previous chapter. Why God should have made us His children is incomprehensible. It shows forth the riches of His grace. John says behold, calling attention as to some wonderful exhibition. What surpassing excellence is this divine love. It is this divine love that will transform believers into the similitude of Christ at Christ's return.

3.3 And every man that hath this hope in him purifieth himself, even as he is pure.

3.3 Purifieth. To purify is to make clean. If the believer will make himself clean, God's love will bestow divine purity on the believer.

3.4-6 Whosoever committeth sin transgresseth also the law: for sin is the transgression of the law. 5 And ye know that he was manifested to take away our sins; and in him is no sin. 6 Whosoever abideth in him sinneth not: whosoever sinneth hath not seen him, neither known him.

3.4-6 Sin. John turns from divine purity and divine love to the consequence of sin. Jesus was manifested to take away sin. The commission of sin denies Christ the purpose of His mission on earth. The believer who abides in Christ does not sin, for light and darkness, good and evil cannot coexist. To abide in Christ is to be the vine while he is the branch. Life comes from him. Sin is the admission that the believer is false and has not experienced Christ as the branch. Christ the branch provides light, life, grace, holiness, wisdom, strength, joy, peace and comfort.

3.7-8 Little children, let no man deceive you: he that doeth righteousness is righteous, even as he is righteous. 8 He that committeth sin is of the devil; for the devil sinneth from the beginning. For this purpose the Son of God was manifested, that he might destroy the works of the devil.

3.7-8 The devil. John strongly states the cause and effect of sin. Sin is of the devil. Christ came to destroy the works of the devil. Actions and manner of living prove allegiance. Those who sin declare an allegiance to the devil. Those who live righteous lives declare allegiance to Christ.

3.9-10 Whosoever is born of God doth not commit sin; for his seed remaineth in him: and he cannot sin, because he is born of God. 10 In this the children of God are manifest, and the children of the devil: whosoever doeth not righteousness is not of God, neither he that loveth not his brother.

3.9-10 Manifest. John does not teach sinless perfection. John is speaking of habitual and known sinful acts. A true believer will conform his character to Christ, this will be reflected in his behavior. Actions declare who is a child of God and who is a child of the devil. Who a believer imitates, whose will the believer does, these declare who the father is.

3.11-12 For this is the message that ye heard from the beginning, that we should love one another. 12 Not as Cain, who was of that wicked one, and slew his brother. And wherefore slew he him? Because his own works were evil, and his brother's righteous.

3.11-12 Love. The chiefest action of proof is love toward one another. John again illustrates by the contrast. To illustrate true love he holds up the opposite, Cain. Cain's actions revealed who his father was. Cain was of that wicked one, the devil. Cain showed the disposition and influence of the devil when he killed his brother.

3.13-15 Marvel not, my brethren, if the world hate you. 14 We know that we have passed from death unto life,

because we love the brethren. He that loveth not his brother abideth in death. 15 Whosoever hateth his brother is a murderer: and ye know that no murderer hath eternal life abiding in him.

3.13-15 Contrast. John again contrasts the opposites of love and hate. John uses this technique more effectively than any Bible author. He uses life and death to show the polar opposites of love and hate. He likens hate to murder and the absence of eternal life. This is classic John. Simple, direct words speaking profound meanings. This is a powerful passage to show disposition is more important than the act itself. Without the rancor, the act would never happen. John is reaching for the fountain head of sin rather than just the acts of committed sin.

3.16-18 Hereby perceive we the love of God, because he laid down his life for us: and we ought to lay down our lives for the brethren. 17 But whoso hath this world's good, and seeth his brother have need, and shutteth up his bowels of compassion from him, how dwelleth the love of God in him? 18 My little children, let us not love in word, neither in tongue; but in deed and in truth.

3.16-18 Intent. John presents the example of Jesus giving His life. This was the intent of God before the foundation of the world. If a believer will have the correct intent, the correct actions will flow as a natural effect. We are admonished to love and have compassion. If these are matters of intent before we encounter the needs of others, our actions will reflect the love of God. If intent is absent, then our actions may be sensual or carnal. Prayer and fasting prepare us to have Christian intent. Jesus prepared himself for forty days and nights before beginning his actions of ministry. This time of wilderness preparation postured Jesus to always act correctly. Our deeds reveal the intent of our heart.

3.19-24 And hereby we know that we are of the truth, and shall assure our hearts before him. 20 For if our heart condemn us, God is greater than our heart, and knoweth all things. 21 Beloved, if our heart condemn us not, then have we confidence toward God. 22 And whatsoever we ask, we receive of him, because we keep his commandments, and do those things that are pleasing in his sight. 23 And this is his commandment, That we should believe on the name of his Son Jesus Christ, and love one another, as he gave us commandment. 24 And he that keepeth his commandments dwelleth in him, and he in him. And hereby we know that he abideth in us, by the Spirit which he hath given us.

3.19-24 Hearts. Our intent produces the actions that assure us before God. Right actions reveal truth on the inside. When our heart does not condemn (find fault with) us, we have confidence (assurance) toward God. Condemnation is always about self. Our confidence toward God rests in following the two greatest commandments of loving God, and loving our fellow man. Our confidence is strong when we ask things of God because we are absent of self motive. Our intent is pure. Doing whatever God wants us to do is easy and helping others becomes a joy. If you have the right intent, submission to God is never an issue.

Chapter 4

4.1-3 Beloved, believe not every spirit, but try the spirits whether they are of God: because many false prophets are gone out into the world. 2 Hereby know ye the Spirit of God: Every spirit that confesseth that Jesus Christ is come in the flesh is of God: 3 And every spirit that confesseth not that Jesus Christ is come in the flesh is not of God: and this is that spirit of antichrist, whereof ye have heard that it should come; and even now already is it in the world.

4.1-3 Spirits. John continues to expound on the source of sin and evil. The results were easily seen in the attacks the church were experiencing. By revealing the source of the evil as spirits, the battle can be engaged and won. To battle the actions without cutting off the intent will only prolong the carnage. The source of sin and evil is spiritual. The test of what spirit is at the root of any action is, does that spirit confess that Jesus Christ has come in the flesh? This is a direct attack on the spirit of Gnosticism. John singles out the spirit of Gnosticism as the spirit of antichrist.

4.3-6 And every spirit that confesseth not that Jesus Christ is come in the flesh is not of God: and this is

that spirit of antichrist, whereof ye have heard that it should come; and even now already is it in the world. 4 Ye are of God, little children, and have overcome them: because greater is he that is in you, than he that is in the world. 5 They are of the world: therefore speak they of the world, and the world heareth them. 6 We are of God: he that knoweth God heareth us; he that is not of God heareth not us. Hereby know we the spirit of truth, and the spirit of error.

4.3-6 Spirt of truth and error. John clearly points out both truth and error are fueled by spirits. It is the intent behind each of these spirits that reveal their source. True believers have the spirit of Jesus Christ while false believers have the spirit of antichrist. Possibly there was some frustration that these false believers were not hearing John's admonitions. He again raises the intent issue. If their intent is to hear truth they will hear him. If their intent is wrong they will not hear him. The spirit of truth and the spirit of error are defined by the intent of the believer. If a believer hears John's instruction, then they are of the spirit of truth. If they discard John's instruction, they are of the spirit of error. John's style of contrasting two ideas is bold and decisive and leaves no room for gray, obscure areas. They are plain words but they are easily understood.

4.7-11 Beloved, let us love one another: for love is of God; and every one that loveth is born of God, and knoweth God. 8 He that loveth not knoweth not God; for God is love. 9 In this was manifested the love of God toward us, because that God sent his only begotten Son into the world, that we might live through him. 10 Herein is love, not that we loved God, but that he loved us, and sent his Son to be the propitiation for

our sins. 11 Beloved, if God so loved us, we ought also to love one another.

4.7-11 Love. The outward demonstration of love shows the believer has the same intent as Jesus Christ. If love is not manifest from the heart of the believer, the believer does not know God. The mark of loving your neighbor as yourself grows out of being born of God. If a person does not love, they do not know God. God showed His intent by love. God so loved the world he gave His only begotten Son. Love gives so others are bettered. Because God loved, God gave, because God gave, we live. Love is not proved because we love God. Love is proved because God loved us. This is the pattern for the believer. Love others. Do not wait until they love you. Follow the intent of God by loving others first. We ought (to be under obligation, to owe), also to love one another.

4.12-14 No man hath seen God at any time. If we love one another, God dwelleth in us, and his love is perfected in us. 13 Hereby know we that we dwell in him, and he in us, because he hath given us of his Spirit. 14 And we have seen and do testify that the Father sent the Son to be the Saviour of the world.

4.12-14 Love in action. The action of love shows the world the God they cannot see. No man hath seen God, but men can see the intent of God through acts of love to other people. Love is a language all it's own. Love needs no words. Love needs no interpretation. Love never needs explaining. Love is the purest example of God man can display. God loved us. We see this by His sacrifice of His son. To love one another is to perfect the love of God in ourself.

4.15-19 Whosoever shall confess that Jesus is the Son of God, God dwelleth in him, and he in God. 16 And we have known and believed the love that God hath to us. God is love; and he that dwelleth in love dwelleth in God, and God in him. 17 Herein is our love made perfect, that we may have boldness in the day of judgment: because as he is, so are we in this world. 18 There is no fear in love; but perfect love casteth out fear: because fear hath torment. He that feareth is not made perfect in love. 19 We love him, because he first loved us.

4.15-19. Perfect love. To confess (to assent, to covenant) that Jesus is the son of God proves the believer is of God. The inner intent reveals the action. The believer follows the pattern and example God sets of love others first. This is to dwell in God, for God is love. He that dwelleth in love, dwelleth in God. The simplicity of this is profound. Countless people have sought to know how to dwell in God. The answer is simple yet profound. John uses simple words to reveal this profound truth. To dwell in God, love others. This is when love is made perfect and God lives in the believer. This intent produces boldness (confidence) in the day of judgment, because as He is, so are we in this world. The pattern is set. We love Him because He first loved us. We must love first, and never wait for others to love us first. The epitome of hypocrisy is the claim to love God while withholding love from others.

4.20-21 If a man say, I love God, and hateth his brother, he is a liar: for he that loveth not his brother whom he hath seen, how can he love God whom he hath not seen? 21 And this commandment have we from him, That he who loveth God love his brother also.

4.20-21 Hate. John closes this line of thought with a final contrast to illuminate true love. John holds up hate. The image is stark and ugly. Coming on the heels of the last illumination of true love and the power of God's love, hate is revealed as the scourge it is. Into the light of brilliant love and hope, John holds up the antithesis and the image is etched forever in the mind of the believer. This moment ties all of love together. To love is to be of God. To hate is to be a liar. Love and hate, light and darkness, truth and liar, the seen and the unseen, the intent and the action, the illumination is stellar.

Chapter 5

5.1 Whosoever believeth that Jesus is the Christ is born of God: and every one that loveth him that begat loveth him also that is begotten of him.

5.1 Believe. The New Testament is clear on what it means to believe. Believing brings action. It is never passive, but it is always active. To believe on Jesus Christ brings action. It means repenting, being baptized and receiving the baptism of the Holy Ghost. (Acts 2, 8, 10, and 19). When a person has biblically believed by being born again of water and spirit (Jn 3.1-7), he is born of God.

5.2-3 By this we know that we love the children of God, when we love God, and keep his commandments. 3 For this is the love of God, that we keep his commandments: and his commandments are not grievous.

5.2-3 Love. Love is also an active entity. John exhorts that when we love God we do something. Love produces action. We keep His commandments. This is the love of God that we keep His commandments. His commandments are not grievous (burdensome). Love and obedience are inseparable.

5.4-5 For whatsoever is born of God overcometh the world: and this is the victory that overcometh the world, even our faith. 5 Who is he that overcometh the world, but he that believeth that Jesus is the Son of God.

5.4-5 Overcome. Jesus Christ overcame the world. When someone is born of God they also overcome (subdue) the world. This is the natural process of believing. It should be natural for a child of God to overcome the world. Believing produces victory through obedience.

5.6-8 This is he that came by water and blood, even Jesus Christ; not by water only, but by water and blood. And it is the Spirit that beareth witness, because the Spirit is truth. 7 For there are three that bear record in heaven, the Father, the Word, and the Holy Ghost: and these three are one. 8 And there are three that bear witness in earth, the Spirit, and the water, and the blood: and these three agree in one.

5.6-8 Witness. John is presenting his witness for Jesus Christ. He presents water and blood as sure witnesses. He declares there are three that bear record in heaven, and these witnesses are sure. He declares The witnesses on earth as well. Heaven and earth, the water and the blood all agree Jesus Christ is the savior of the world.

5.9-10 If we receive the witness of men, the witness of God is greater: for this is the witness of God which he hath testified of his Son. 10 He that believeth on the Son of God hath the witness in himself: he that believeth not God hath made him a liar; because he believeth not the record that God gave of his Son.

5.9-10 Ibid. The witnesses John presented are true. The witness of men is true, the witness of God is greater. God himself witnesses of Jesus Christ. There is no more powerful voice of truth than the Father himself. The Gnostics had no witnesses for their damnable doctrine. John presents witnesses from heaven and earth, and then the star witness, God himself. If this array of witnesses is not believed, that person is a liar. To deny the biblical witness of Christ is to reject God himself.

5.11-12 And this is the record, that God hath given to us eternal life, and this life is in his Son. 12 He that hath the Son hath life; and he that hath not the Son of God hath not life.

5.11-12 Life. This is the record. God hath given us eternal life and that life is in Jesus Christ. The simple fact is if you have Jesus Christ you have life. If you do not have the Son of God you do not have life. Your believing requires action to be valid.

5.13-15 These things have I written unto you that believe on the name of the Son of God; that ye may know that ye have eternal life, and that ye may believe on the name of the Son of God. 14 And this is the confidence that we have in him, that, if we ask any thing according to his will, he heareth us: 15 And if we know that he hear us, whatsoever we ask, we know that we have the petitions that we desired of him.

5.13-15 Name. The assurance of a believer is not based on feeling, but on the principals of God's Word. These principals include obedience, believing, and loving the brethren. These things bring an inner witness of the

Spirit of God. It is this assurance that leads to confidence in prayer. We know we have the petitions we ask of God.

5.16-21 If any man see his brother sin a sin which is not unto death, he shall ask, and he shall give him life for them that sin not unto death. There is a sin unto death: I do not say that he shall pray for it. 17 All unrighteousness is sin: and there is a sin not unto death. 18 We know that whosoever is born of God sinneth not; but he that is begotten of God keepeth himself, and that wicked one toucheth him not. 19 And we know that we are of God, and the whole world lieth in wickedness. 20 And we know that the Son of God is come, and hath given us an understanding, that we may know him that is true, and we are in him that is true, even in his Son Jesus Christ. This is the true God, and eternal life. 21 Little children, keep yourselves from idols. Amen.

5.16-21 Sin. These final words are written to encourage the believers about what John has written in this epistle. The sin unto death is not believing in Jesus Christ. Anyone not believing in Jesus Christ will be lost. The sin not unto death are sins that do not mark deliberate and persistent rebellion against God. All believers must use caution to not fall into these sins. These sins are not apostasy from biblical truth or failure to trust in Christ. Living in faith and obedience puts the believer beyond the touch of Satan. John issues a final note of assurance. We are of God and the whole world lieth in wickedness. Believers have believed in the true God, Jesus Christ. The final charge is to keep yourself from idols. The love and devotion of believers is to be toward Jesus Christ only. Any other love equates to worshipping idols.

2 John

Introduction. Every generation has faced unique circumstances in the spread of the gospel of Jesus Christ. This was evident in the years 2 John was penned. Travel was convenient due to the great system of Roman roads. These roads made travel easier. There were still dangers of robbers and thieves, but the travel was common and frequent. This posed an opportunity for false teachers to circulate among New Testament believers easily. To add to the problem of leaven (false doctrine), entering the church, was where a traveler would lodge. There were no modern hotels as we know them today. There were occasional Inns. It was common for the family of God in the New Testament to lodge with believers. There was a network that traveling believers utilized to travel safely and also have fellowship with other believers. This presented a golden opportunity for false teachers to gain access into the privacy of believers homes under the guise of a brother. This problem had become so prevalent that the aged apostle John was summoned by the Holy Spirit to write a warning of this spreading spiritual malaise. False teachers such as the Gnostics hit the circuit and spread their false doctrine. Other people used the homes of believers for free food and lodging while posing as a believer.

2 John and 3 John address this situation. They are short letters of instruction to guide the church in these matters in the closing years of the first century. The church had been around now for approximately 60 years and these practical teachings were increasingly necessary. 2 John is addressed to a particular lady who was generous in her providing food and lodging to traveling believers. The aged Apostle John is instructing how to discern between the true believer and an imposter. It is love and obedience that define a true believer.

Date: 90 ad

Author: John the Apostle

Place: Ephesus

Chapter 1

1.1 The elder unto the elect lady and her children, whom I love in the truth; and not I only, but also all they that have known the truth;

1.1 Author. John does not identify himself as the author. This follows his practice established in his gospel. He is confident those reading this short epistle will know who the elder is. The elect lady here is not identified by name. Apparently she was also well known and needed no name mentioned to distinguish her. Her fame and reputation had gone throughout the community of believers of the first century.

1.2 For the truth's sake, which dwelleth in us, and shall be with us for ever.

1.2 Truth. As in his other epistles, there is a priority on truth in all John's writings. Truth is the signal identifier of true believers. It is the trademark of Christianity. This letter is written for the truth's sake.

1.3 Grace be with you, mercy, and peace, from God the Father, and from the Lord Jesus Christ, the Son of the Father, in truth and love.

1.3 Blessing. It was common practice for an Apostle to give blessings upon the believer. Here John offers grace, mercy, peace to the believers. This practice is well documented in New Testament history. We see this in writings of the Apostle Paul in particular.

1.4 I rejoiced greatly that I found of thy children walking in truth, as we have received a commandment from the Father.

1.4 Rejoiced. John rejoiced (happy, cheerful) greatly (exceedingly) when he saw the false teachers circulating though the fellowship of believers had not had influence on this lady or her children. It gave the aged Apostle great joy to know the formula for successful Christian living was working. Obedience, love, and intent were producing the correct result in her life and in the lives of her children. No doubt this thrilled John and gave assurance the gospel would indeed triumph over false insurgents of the faith. What a feeling of contentment must have surged through John at this confirmation of the power of the gospel. Walking in truth is a Jewish idiom for living in truth. This lady and her children were living epistles, known and read of all men. This was a living example of the gospel enduring attack and being victorious. John may have mused over the day Jesus said the gates of hell shall not prevail against the church. John was watching this statement come true through this lady and her children. John had given his life for this gospel and it caused great rejoicing to see it triumph over the leaven of false doctrine.

1.5 And now I beseech thee, lady, not as though I wrote a new commandment unto thee, but that

which we had from the beginning, that we love one another.

1.5 Love. John was assured of her victory, so he now returns to the commandment he had preached for so many years. John was in his late eighties or nineties at the time of this writing. He lived in Ephesus and had to be carried to the church on a litter. He was known for waving from the litter and speaking the phrase love one another. John speaks of love almost as much as all the other gospel writers combined. John knew love would overcome any obstacle. He lovingly reminds the elect lady that love is the primary Christian commandment.

1.6 And this is love, that we walk after his commandments. This is the commandment, That, as ye have heard from the beginning, ye should walk in it.

1.6 Walk. John reminds the elect lady and his readers of this epistle, that love is active. Love produces action in our lives. When we love God we walk in His commandments. This is the evidence of love, how we live and how we walk. Jesus had taught this principal many times, Jn 14.15, 21, 23, 24, 15.10, 14.

1.7 For many deceivers are entered into the world, who confess not that Jesus Christ is come in the flesh. This is a deceiver and an antichrist.

1.7 Deceivers. John again declares warnings about Gnostics and pseudo-Christians who are deceivers (roving impostors). These impostors claimed Jesus never came in the flesh. This attack on the incarnation of Christ was an attack at the very foundation of Christianity. John declares this is the spirit of antichrist.

1.8 Look to yourselves, that we lose not those things which we have wrought, but that we receive a full reward.

1.8 Reward. This is an important verse. John shows the concern that things can be lost through time. John wanted the next generation of believers to not lose anything in transition. It was obvious many changes had occurred in the last half century and John is advocating for every generation to receive full reward (wages).

1.9 Whosoever transgresseth, and abideth not in the doctrine of Christ, hath not God. He that abideth in the doctrine of Christ, he hath both the Father and the Son.

1.9 Transgression. John returns to central themes he has recorded in 1 John, which was written at the same time. The consensus is your life proves who you are. If sin is dominant and you do not abide (remain), you do not have God in you. The Christian life is more than words, it is action. True religion causes people to live right and proves their inner experience with God. This theme is prominent in all three of John's later day epistles.

1.10 If there come any unto you, and bring not this doctrine, receive him not into your house, neither bid him God speed:

1.10 Doctrine. The qualifier was the doctrine. It was

not about status or finance or popularity. John boldly instructed her to refuse lodging and food to any who did not bring this doctrine. This may seem harsh at first glance, but when the final conclusion is eternal life is at stake, this seems a rational measure.

1.11 For he that biddeth him God speed is partaker of his evil deeds.

1.11 Partaker. This is a challenging concept. To be a partaker is to share in their purpose and success. To bid means to have discourse, an extended harangue. It appears John is aligning himself with other New Testament teachings to not indulge in questions and discussion with these false teachers. They are not to be treated as harmless. They are to be dissed and ignored. There doctrine is leaven to the truth of the gospel and future generations must have the pure doctrine passed to them. Paul went so far as to say let them be accursed, Gal 1.8-9.

1.12-13 Having many things to write unto you, I would not write with paper and ink: but I trust to come unto you, and speak face to face, that our joy may be full. 13 The children of thy elect sister greet thee. Amen.

1.12-13 Papyrus. John is writing on papyrus, a writing material made from reeds. He instructs he has many things to communicate but would rather speak to them face to face. The times demanded the apostle be vigilant and unceasing in his defense of the gospel. His voice was the last vestment of original Apostolic instruction. Soon the audible voices would be silent. The New Testament era would close and be forever handed to the eternal. His writings will never lose their voice and give us guidance today as they did in AD 90.

3 John

Introduction. This short epistle is a companion book to 2 John. In 2 John, the Elder, John, had warned against entertaining false teachers. In this short personal letter he applauds a man named Gaius for warmly welcoming genuine Christian leaders. These Christian acts had been criticized by a man named Diotrephes who was also gossiping against John. These two letters 2 John and 3 John deal with heresy and church splits. This has proven to be a recurring problem in every generation. Though small, these two books are important in teaching believers how to deal with these two factions of error that arise in any church. John gives the remedy for these dangers. He urges love and discernment. Believers must know whom to accept and whom to reject. Welcome true believers with open arms and hospitality. Close the door of welcome and fellowship to all who deny Jesus Christ as having come in the flesh.

Author: John the Apostle

Date: 90AD

Place: Ephesus

1.1 The elder unto the wellbeloved Gaius, whom I love in the truth.

1.1 Wellbeloved. What an honor to be called wellbeloved by John. Gaius must have been extraordinary or have earned this level of honor and respect. John had known all the members of the early church. To receive this moniker speaks multitudes of Gaius. John loves him in the truth. John again sets the criteria for fellowship and hospitality. Gaius has been faithful to the truth. The truth was too valuable to John to trust it to unfaithful men.

1.2 Beloved, I wish above all things that thou mayest prosper and be in health, even as thy soul prospereth.

1.2 Health. John wishes for Gaius' health to be as whole as his spiritual health. John is showing the Christian love he teaches others to have. The greatest teachers are those who live their creeds.

1.3 For I rejoiced greatly, when the brethren came and testified of the truth that is in thee, even as thou walkest in the truth.

1.3 Truth. John rejoices in things that are eternal. Truth never dies. When John received the news of Gaius love for truth it caused him to rejoice. True leaders value their disciples maintaining truth above all other characteristics.

1.4 I have no greater joy than to hear that my children walk in truth.

1.4 Joy. The joy John experienced was to know that truth was being passed on to the next generation. Rejoiced here means to be full of cheer. There must have been a big smile that crossed John's face when informed of Gaius' love for the truth.

1.5 Beloved, thou doest faithfully whatsoever thou doest to the brethren, and to strangers;

1.5 Faithfully. John's commendation means Gaius was trustworthy. Gaius had not just been faithful to the brethren, but also to strangers or guests. The issue in this letter is the same as 2 John. The issue is when and how to entertain people who claim to be New Testament believers. In this Gaius had excelled.

1.6 Which have borne witness of thy charity before the church: whom if thou bring forward on their journey after a godly sort, thou shalt do well:

1.6 Charity. Gaius charity (love) had been witnessed by those who had been the beneficiary of his love. Gaius was a living example of John's life long sermon about love one another. Gaius charity had now been spoken of in the church.

1.7 Because that for his name's sake they went forth, taking nothing of the Gentiles.

1.7 Gain. The name of Jesus had provided a fellowship of believers so that the travelers did not have to receive anything from Gentiles who were not part of the church.

1.8 We therefore ought to receive such, that we might be fellowhelpers to the truth.

1.8 Receive. John is encouraging the church and Gaius to receive these believers and assist them in the love of Jesus Christ. To help these travelers was to help the truth. This reflects back to when Jesus told his disciples when you do this unto the least of these you do it unto me, Mt 25.40.

1.9-10 I wrote unto the church: but Diotrephes, who loveth to have the preeminence among them, receiveth us not. 10 Wherefore, if I come, I will remember his deeds which he doeth, prating against us with malicious words: and not content therewith, neither doth he himself receive the brethren, and forbiddeth them that would, and casteth them out of the church.

1.9-10 Diotrephes. Diotrephes was a gentile whose name means brought up by Jupiter. This man loved the preeminence (being first). John had written unto the church but Diotrephes must have not received John's communique. It must have gone so far as prating (babbler) speaking malicious (hurtful) words against John. Diotrephes was not content (to raise a barrier). This dissenter was creating division in the church. He was not receiving the brethren and was forbidding those that would. This is an egregious affront to the truth John is teaching and advocating about love. Diotrephes had actually cast people from the church when they followed the teaching of John.

1.11 Beloved, follow not that which is evil, but that

which is good. He that doeth good is of God: but he that doeth evil hath not seen God.

1.11 Evil. John plainly says these kind of acts by Diotrephes are evil (worthless, depraved). John is using his Apostolic position to plainly say do not follow this kind of division in the church. He that doeth good is of God, he that doeth evil hath not seen God, is a strong indictment against Diotrephes.

1.12 Demetrius hath good report of all men, and of the truth itself: yea, and we also bear record; and ye know that our record is true.

1.12 Demetrius. John now directs the church to follow Demetrius who has a good report of all men, but more importantly of the truth itself. John gives his endorsement of Demetrius and appeals to his own reputation as being true.

1.13-14 I had many things to write, but I will not with ink and pen write unto thee: 14 But I trust I shall shortly see thee, and we shall speak face to face. Peace be to thee. Our friends salute thee. Greet the friends by name.

1.13-14 John concludes by letting them know he has more to say, but chooses not to write these things down but will speak when they are together. John encourages Gaius to greet the friends by name. The family of believers were dear to each other and John sends his greetings. This letter and the epistle of James are the only epistles to conclude without amen.

www.ingramcontent.com/pod-product-compliance
Lightning Source LLC
Chambersburg PA
CBHW040326300426
44112CB00021B/2888